Five Little Ducks

and Other Action Rhymes

10

Zita Newcome

Yuji

Jordan

Melissa

Rosie

Yasmin

Charlie

Sam

Anna

Angelina

For Claire –
my ever-inspiring singing partner

First published 1997 by Walker Books Ltd
87 Vauxhall Walk, London SE11 5HJ

This edition published 2002

2 4 6 8 10 9 7 5 3

This collection and *Down at the Bottom*
of the Deep Blue Sea © 1997 Zita Newcome

Printed in Hong Kong

British Library Cataloguing in Publication Data:
a catalogue record for this book is
available from the British Library

ISBN 0-7445-8917-7

Contents

The Wheels On the Bus

The wheels on the bus
go round and round,
Round and round,
round and round,
The wheels on the bus
go round and round,
All day long.

The wipers on the bus go
swish, swish, swish . . .

The horn on the bus goes
beep! beep! beep! . . .

The people on the bus go
chat, chat, chat . . .

The children on the bus
bump up and down . . .

4

round and round,

swish, swish, swish,

beep! beep! bee

The babies on the bus go
"WAAH! WAAH! WAAH!" . . .

The grannies on the bus go
knit, knit, knit . . .

The wheels on the bus go
round and round,
All day long.

chat, chat,

bump up and down,

WAAH! WAAH!

knit, knit, knit,

I'm a Little Teapot

I'm a little teapot, short and stout,
Here's my handle, here's my spout.
When I see the teacups, hear me shout:
Tip me up and pour me out!

I'm a tube of toothpaste on the shelf,
I get so lonely all by myself,
When it comes to night-time, hear me shout:
Lift my lid off and squeeze me out!

Here's my handle,
here's my spout.

Tip me up and
pour me out!

I'm a tube of
toothpaste . . .

Lift my lid off
and

squeeze me out!

Pat-a-cake

Pat-a-cake, pat-a-cake, baker's man,
Bake me a cake as fast as you can.
Pat it and prick it and mark it with B,
And put it in the oven for baby and me.

Pat-a-cake,
pat-a-cake . . .

Pat it

and prick it and
mark it with B,

And put it in the
oven for baby
and me.

*Tickle as you
say the last line.*

7

Head, Shoulders, Knees and Toes

Sing slow, then fast

Head, shoulders, knees and toes, knees and toes,
Head, shoulders, knees and toes, knees and toes,
And eyes and ears and mouth and nose,
Head, shoulders, knees and toes, knees and toes.

Five Little Monkeys

Five little
monkeys . . .

Five little monkeys jumping on the bed,
One fell off and bumped his head,
Mummy phoned the doctor and the doctor said,
"No more monkeys jumping on the bed!"

Four little monkeys . . .
Three little monkeys . . .
Two little monkeys . . .
One little monkey . . .

and bumped
his head,

Mummy phoned
the doctor . . .

"No more monkeys
jumping on
the bed!"

*Repeat actions
showing one less
finger each time,
as you count
down.*

9

Miss Polly Had a Dolly

Miss Polly had a dolly who was sick, sick, sick,
So she called for the doctor to come quick, quick, quick,
The doctor came with his bag and his hat,
And he knocked on the door with a rat-a-tat-tat,

He looked at the dolly and he shook his head,
And he said, "Miss Polly, put her straight to bed."
He wrote on a paper for a pill, pill, pill,
"I'll be back in the morning with my bill, bill, bill."

Teddy Bear, Teddy Bear

Teddy bear, teddy bear, touch your nose,
Teddy bear, teddy bear, touch your toes,
Teddy bear, teddy bear, touch the ground,
Teddy bear, teddy bear, turn around.

Teddy bear, teddy bear, climb the stairs,
Teddy bear, teddy bear, say your prayers,
Teddy bear, teddy bear, turn out the light,
Teddy bear, teddy bear, say goodnight!

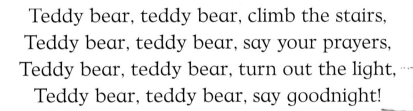

Little Peter Rabbit

Little Peter Rabbit had a fly upon his nose.
Little Peter Rabbit had a fly upon his nose.
Little Peter Rabbit had a fly upon his nose.
And he swished it and he swashed it
And the fly flew away.

Little Peter
Rabbit

had a fly upon
his nose.

And he swished it
and he swashed it

Powder puff and

curly whiskers,

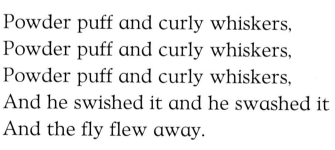

Powder puff and curly whiskers,
Powder puff and curly whiskers,
Powder puff and curly whiskers,
And he swished it and he swashed it
And the fly flew away.

12

Little Miss Muffet

Little Miss Muffet, sat on her tuffet,
Eating her curds and whey.
There came a big spider,
Who sat down beside her,
And frightened Miss Muffet away!

Little Miss Muffet,
sat on her tuffet,

Eating her curds
and whey.

There came a
big spider . . .

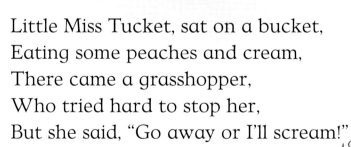

Little Miss Tucket, sat on a bucket,
Eating some peaches and cream,
There came a grasshopper,
Who tried hard to stop her,
But she said, "Go away or I'll scream!"

And frightened
Miss Muffet away!

"Go away or
I'll scream!"

13

Round and Round the Garden

Round and round the garden,
Like a teddy bear,

One step, two step,

Tickle you under there!

Mouse In a Hole

A mouse lived in a little hole,
Lived softly in a little hole,
When all was quiet, as quiet as can be . . .

OUT POPPED HE!

There Was a Little Turtle

There was a little turtle,

He lived in a box.

He swam in a puddle,

He climbed on the rocks

He snapped at a mosquito,
He snapped at a flea.
He snapped at a minnow,
He snapped at me.

He caught the mosquito,
He caught the flea.
He caught the minnow,

But . . . he didn't catch me!

15

Incey Wincey Spider

Incey Wincey Spider
Climbed up . . .

Down came
the rain

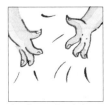

And washed poor
Incey out.

Out came the sun,

Repeat first action
as you sing last
line of the rhyme.

Incey Wincey Spider
Climbed up the water spout.
Down came the rain
And washed poor Incey out.
Out came the sun,
And dried up all the rain.
So Incey Wincey Spider
Climbed up the spout again.

16

I Hear Thunder

I hear thunder, I hear thunder,
Hark don't you? Hark don't you?
Pitter patter raindrops, pitter patter raindrops,
I'm wet through, so are you!

I see blue skies, I see blue skies,
Way up high, way up high,
Hurry up the sunshine, hurry up the sunshine,
We'll soon dry, we'll soon dry.

I hear thunder . . .

Pitter patter
raindrops,

. . . I see blue skies,
Way up high . . .

We'll soon dry,
we'll soon dry.

17

Oats and Beans and Barley Grow

Oats and beans
and barley grow,

First the farmer
sows his seed,

Then he stands
and takes his ease.

And turns around
to view the land.

Oats and beans and barley grow,
Oats and beans and barley grow,
And not you, nor I, nor anyone know,
How oats and beans and barley grow.

First the farmer sows his seed,
Then he stands and takes his ease.
He stamps his feet and claps his hands
And turns around to view the land.

Oats and beans and barley grow . . .

Dingle Dangle Scarecrow

When all the cows were sleeping
And the sun had gone to bed,
Up jumped the scarecrow
And this is what he said:

I'm a dingle dangle scarecrow
With a flippy floppy hat!
I can shake my arms like this,
I can shake my legs like that!

When the cows were in the meadow
And the pigeons in the loft,
Up jumped the scarecrow
And whispered very soft:

I'm a dingle dangle scarecrow . . .

When all the hens were roosting
And the moon behind a cloud,
Up jumped the scarecrow
And shouted very loud:

I'm a dingle dangle scarecrow . . .

I'm a dingle dangle scarecrow

With a flippy floppy hat!

I can shake my arms like this,

I can shake my legs like that!

This Little Piggy

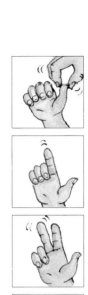

This little piggy went to market,

This little piggy stayed at home,

This little piggy had roast beef,

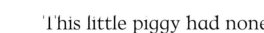

This little piggy had none.

This little piggy went . . .

Wee, wee, wee,
all the way home!

*Run fingers up
arm and tickle!*

Five Little Ducks

Five little ducks went out one day,

Over the hills and far away,

Mother Duck said, "Quack, quack, quack, quack,"

But only four little ducks came back.

Four little ducks went out one day . . .
Three little ducks went out one day . . .
Two little ducks went out one day . . .

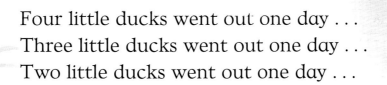

One little duck went out one day,
Over the hills and far away,
Mother Duck said, "Quack, quack, quack, quack,"
And all the five little ducks came back.

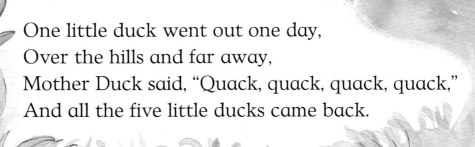

Walking Through the Jungle

Walking through the jungle,
What do you see?
Can you hear a noise?
What could it be?

Ah well, I think it is a snake, Sss! Sss! Sss!
I think it is a snake, Sss! Sss! Sss!
I think it is a snake, Sss! Sss! Sss!
Looking for his tea.

Walking through the jungle . . .
Ah well, I think it is a tiger, Roar! Roar! Roar! . . .

Walking through the jungle,

What do you see?

Can you hear a noise?

What could it be?

I think it is a snake . . .

Looking for his tea.

Walking through the jungle . . .
Ah well, I think it is a monkey, Ooo! Ooo! Ooo! . . .

Walking through the jungle . . .
Ah well, I think it is an elephant, Stomp! Stomp! Stomp! . . .

Walking through the jungle . . .

Ah well, I think it is a crocodile, Snap! Snap! Snap!
I think it is a crocodile, Snap! Snap! Snap!
I think it is a crocodile, Snap! Snap! Snap!
Looking for his tea . . .

HOPE IT ISN'T ME!

think it is a
iger . . .

I think it is a
monkey . . .

I think it is an
elephant . . .

I think it is a
crocodile . . .

Looking for
his tea . . .

HOPE IT
ISN'T ME!

Row, Row, Row Your Boat

Row, row, row your boat gently down the stream,
Merrily, merrily, merrily, merrily, life is but a dream.

Rock, rock, rock your boat gently to and fro,
Watch out! Give a shout, into the water you go!

Row, row, row your boat down the jungle stream,
If you see a crocodile, don't forget to scream!

Row, row, row
your boat . . .

Rock, rock, rock
your boat . . .

. . . into the
water you go!

. . . don't forget
to scream!

Mr Crocodile

Three little monkeys swinging from a tree,
Teasing Mr Crocodile, "You can't catch me!"
Along came Mr Crocodile, quiet as can be . . . SNAP!

Two little monkeys swinging from a tree,
Teasing Mr Crocodile, "You can't catch me!"
Along came Mr Crocodile, quiet as can be . . . SNAP!

One little monkey swinging from a tree,
Teasing Mr Crocodile, "You can't catch me!"
Along came Mr Crocodile, quiet as can be,
SNAP! . . . "MISSED ME!"

Three little
monkeys

swinging from
a tree,

Teasing Mr
Crocodile . . .

. . . SNAP!

"MISSED ME!"

25

The Elephant

The elephant goes like this, like that,
He's terribly big, and he's terribly fat.
He has no fingers, he has no toes,
But goodness gracious, what a nose!

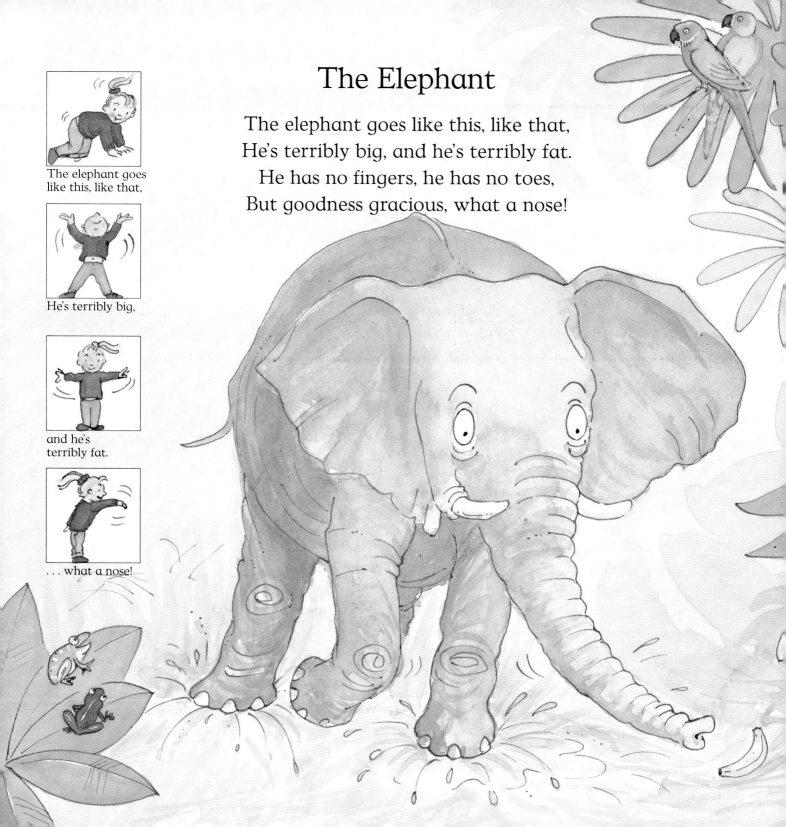

The elephant goes
like this, like that,

He's terribly big,

and he's
terribly fat.

. . . what a nose!

Boa Constrictor

I'm being eaten by a boa constrictor,
A boa constrictor, a boa constrictor,
I'm being eaten by a boa constrictor,
And I don't like it one little bit!

Oh no! He's up to my toe,
Oh gee! He's up to my knee,
Oh fiddle! He's up to my middle,
Oh heck! He's up to my neck,
Oh dread! He's over my head!
GULP!

Oh no! He's
up to my toe,

Oh gee! He's
up to my knee,

Oh fiddle! He's
up to my middle,

Oh heck! He's
up to my neck,

Oh dread! He's
over my head!

27

Here is the Sea

Here is the sea, the wavy sea.

Here is a boat, and here is me.

And all the fishes down below,

Wriggle their tails and away they go.

One, Two, Three, Four, Five

One, two,
Three, four, five,

Once I caught a fish alive.

Six, seven,
Eight, nine, ten,

Then I let him go again.

Why did you let him go?
Because he bit my finger so.

Which finger did he bite?
This little finger on the right.

Down at the Bottom of the Deep Blue Sea

*Use your hands and arms to do the actions
described for each sea creature*

Swim swim swim,
swim with me . . .

. . . what will
we see?

Down to the
bottom . . .

Down at the bottom of the deep blue sea,
There's a great big octopus waving at me,
A friendly sting-ray gently flaps by,
And two grey dolphins leap up to the sky.

*Swim swim swim, swim with me,
Swim swim swim, what will we see?
Swim swim swim, swim with me,
Down to the bottom of the deep blue sea.*

Mermaids comb their hair in the waves,
Seaweed dances in the watery caves,
Eel from his hole, peeps in and out,
And whale makes a fountain come out of his spout.

Swim swim swim, swim with me . . .

Down at the bottom of the deep blue sea,
All the pink shrimps are tickling me,
An orange crab does a sideways crawl,
Lobsters clack their pincers – they're having a ball!

Swim swim swim, swim with me . . .

My Ship Sailed to China

My ship sailed to China,
With a cargo of tea,
All laden with treasures
For you and for me.
They bought me a fan,
Just imagine my bliss,
When I found myself going
Like this, like this, like this.

My ship sailed . . .
(sway as you sing)

They bought
me a fan,

Like this, like this,
like this.

*Repeat four times,
each time adding
the wave of an
arm, a leg, and
nodding your head
until you
are finally waving
both arms and
legs and nodding
your head!*